# THE LITTLE BOOK OF

## Ollie'isms

# THE LITTLE BOOK OF

# *Ollie'*
# *isms*

## Ian Holloway

*With David Clayton*

GreenUmbrella
Publishing

This edition first published in the UK in 2008
By Green Umbrella Publishing

© Green Umbrella Publishing 2008

www.gupublishing.co.uk

Publishers: Jules Gammond and Vanessa Gardner

Creative Director: Kevin Gardner

Picture Credits: Getty Images and Shutterstock

Robert Segal Representation

Printed and bound by J. H. Haynes & Co. Ltd., Sparkford

ISBN: 978-1-906229-78-8

# THE LITTLE BOOK OF

# Ollie'isms

# Introduction

A lot of the quotes in this book were inspired by my dad. He had a wonderful happiness about him and he loved being in other people's company.

No matter what would happen, he would think of something to say that would make people laugh or smile. He wasn't a comedian, but no matter how life got, he was always generous and was never short of a saying or comment that seemed to make sense of everything, somehow. I grew up with his wit and wisdom and undoubtedly, it left its mark on me, togther with my own take on life, of course.

'I feel like a dog with two dicks', 'Fit as a butcher's dog', 'All cock and ribs', 'Fit as a drover's dog' – just some of his regular analogies, most of which seemed to include a dog for some reason! Even when something bad has happened, I'll think about what dad would probably have said at that moment and it will make me smile.

He'd bring warmth and joy when people needed it most, just by saying something or remembering something fondly and I think that's a gift – I really do.

There is a book of quotes that was published a few years back but it did contain a number of inaccuracies. I didn't know a thing about it and didn't have the chance to say whether I'd been misquoted or misunderstood – I think it suits a lot of people if they can make me sound crazy or interpret what I say so it doesn't actually make any sense – it must make better copy or something.

The quotes in this book are, however, *bona fide* and, where necessary, I've explained why I said what I did at particular times.

There's an old saying that the apple never falls very far from the tree. I didn't fall very far from my dad's tree and there are loads of saying and comments that I remember that I've kept for myself but they make me remember my dad warmly. I hope you enjoy them, too.

Ian Holloway,
July 2008

# THE LITTLE BOOK OF

# -1-

"*I reckon the ball was travelling at 400mph, and I bet it burned the keeper's eyebrows off.*"

**Ollie's typical understated reaction to a QPR goal at Crewe**

# -2-

*"I mean no dis-respect to Donatella (Versace). I'm sure she would not be flattered to hear she looks like Marc Bircham."*

**The question is, who did Ollie offend the most…?**

**Ollie explains:**
"This was to do with Marc Bircham's hair dye. Everywhere we used to go, people used to ask, 'Who's the guy with the bird shit on his head?' He once dyed his hair blue and white to match QPR's colours and I think if you look at pictures of Donatella Versace and Marc, they seem to share the same hairdresser!"

# Ollie'isms

## -3-

*"I've got to get Dan Shittu ready for the Stoke game. I've told him to go to Iceland and ask if he can sit in one of their freezers."*

**No guessing as to what Shittu's problem might have been...**

**Ollie explains:**
"We were struggling – because Dan is so big – to get icepacks to cover the area we needed to cover so I told the physio it would be better if they took him down to an Iceland frozen food store, open up one of their storage freezers and chuck Dan inside!"

# -4-

---

*"There was a spell in the second half when I took my heart off my sleeve and put it in my mouth."*

**As ever, Ollie puts his heart – and sleeve – into his post-match press confrerences**

# *Ollie'* isms

## -5-

*"Right now, everything is going wrong for me – if I fell in a barrel of boobs, I'd come out sucking my thumb!"*

Ollie, keeping abreast of current humour despite his misfortune at the time

# -6-

## *"We're 5-0 down with a minute to go on this one."*

### Ollie's unique way of warning supporters not to expect a victory

**Ollie explains:**
"We were getting hammered and my team wasn't playing very well. I can't remember what the score was and if anything ever happens at home, I use this analogy to my wife. For instance, if we're trying to fill out some kind of form and are struggling with it, I'll say, 'Christ! We're 5-0 down with a minute to go on this one!' Basically, it means, 'How the hell can I sort this out?' The underlying meaning, however, is that the situation is not entirely lost and we can still turn it around."

# Ollie' isms

## -7-

*"When my mum was running our house, when I was a kid, all the money was put into tins. She knew what was in every tin and I know how much I've got in my tin – that's the way we'll run this club."*

**Ollie – unimpressed by QPR's financial housekeeping**

# -8-

*"Do we want women to come and watch? I do, I think they're bloody pretty, prettier than any man I've seen. What do women like? Legs. Our shorts are getting longer. And why can't players lift their shirts up to celebrate? Who is it disrespecting? Ladies like to see a good looking lad with his shirt off. They'd have to go somewhere else though cos all my lot are ugly as hell. "*

**Ollie, considering changing his team's name to Plymouth Gargoyles**

# Ollie'isms

## -9-

*"He's played 150 games for us and that was his first-ever goal. Believe it or not, I said to him at half-time 'are you ever going to score a goal for us?' and he laughed and said: 'Yeah, one day I will!' Within 10 minutes of the restart, he scored – unbelievable!"*

**Ollie helps Paul Connolly breaks his Plymouth duck**

# -10-

*"To the people who booed – boo to you! Come to my house tomorrow and we can fight!"*

No QPR fan turned up, despite
the invitation…

# -11-

*"Twenty thousand people running the club – that's going to have to be one hell of a room they book when they hold their annual general meeting…"*

**Ollie, not impressed by Ebbsfleet's unique fan ownership**

**Ollie explains:**
"At any club, you have a board of directors or a chairman that you have to speak to once a month and it's hard enough convincing them that you're doing things right – imagine having to consult and impress 20,000 people every minute of the day? I still think it's a ridiculous idea."

# -12-

*"It's like putting a snake in a bag, if you don't tie it up, it will wriggle free."*

**Ollie, rattled by transfer rumours**

# *Ollie'* isms

# -13-

*"What the hell the referee saw I
don't know – he ought to go down
to Specsavers."*

**Ollie makes a spectacle of the
official for the day**

# -14-

*"The fat lady hasn't started to sing yet, but she has a mic in her hand."*

**Ollie compares QPR's precarious financial situation to Karaoke at Weight Watchers**

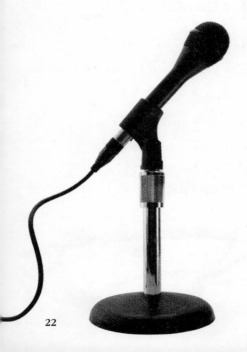

# -15-

*"Has he done it yet? He's got to get his bum cheeks out in Burton's, hasn't he? You can't break a promise, you've got to go there and do it. It won't be a pretty sight, but who cares? Get your butt cheeks out, Gary! That'll put a few Christmas shoppers off, won't it?"*

Ollie reacts to Bristol City manager Gary Johnson's unkept promise to bare his backside in a shop window after losing a bet with Liam Fontaine

# -16-

*"We need a big, ugly defender. If we had one of them we'd have dealt with County's first goal by taking out the ball, the player and the first three rows of seats in the stands."*

Ollie on a defender you wouldn't want to meet in a dark alley…

# -17-

*"You never count your chickens before they hatch. I used to keep parakeets and I never counted every egg thinking I would get all eight birds. You just hoped they came out of the nest box looking all right. I'm like a swan at the moment. I look fine on top of the water but under the water my little legs are going mad."*

**Ollie, paddling his way through this particular problem**

# -18-

*"You can say that strikers are a bit like postmen, they have to get in and out as quick as they can before the dog has a go."*

Ollie puts his own stamp on forwards

# -19-

"Whoever that was, I would like to
pull his pants down and slap his
arse like I used to do to my kids.
Apparently I'm not even allowed to
do that anymore otherwise I will
have the old health and safety on
my back giving it the old
'hello'. The world's gone mad. Tony
Blair won the election, so why's he
gotta resign? I think the
Conservative fella should. If he
couldn't win an election with a
failing government, or a flailing
government, what's the matter with
him? Get out you ain't no good. I

*know we're not talking football...we are, aren't we?"*

**Ollie's classic rant regarding the reporter who claimed Danny Shittu was to be sold – we think**

### Ollie explains:

"I think I was down at Cardiff City at the time and my football team – QPR – had played really well but lost 1-0. I came out and started babbling on about politics. There was a Tory politician who was claiming Tony Blair should resign, despite having just lost an election to him and I just found it all a bit bizarre. At the press conference, people were telling me we should have won and I just said, 'Well that's life, isn't it? But you won't find me going on about it, moaning and saying the other manager should resign – you've just got to get on with it.' I just went off on a tangent because strange things do happen in football, but stranger things happen in life so I was trying to bring a comparison between questions I get asked and questions that Tony Blair might get and the

results he has. Even now, I don't know whether it
made any sense or not, but it did to me – at the
time! I seem to rememeber everyone in the room
being totally perplexed, so I must have done
my job!"

# -20-

*"Our substitute didn't have his shirts or pants on. I've had better days."*

**Ollie on the bare neccessities of life**

# -21-

*"Every dog has its day – and today is woof day! Today I just want to bark."*

**No bone of contention as Ollie celebrates QPR's promotion at Hillsborough**

# -22-

---

*"It's like the film 'Men in Black'. I walk around in a black suit, white shirt and black tie where I've had to flash my white light every now and again to erase some memories, but I feel we've got hold of the galaxy now. It's in our hands."*

**Which planet is Ollie on? Planet Reality, as it happens…**

# Ollie'isms

## -23-

*"When you're a manager it's a case of have suitcase will travel, and I certainly didn't want to travel with my trousers down."*

Ollie always packs his trousers…

# -24-

*"It was lucky that the linesman wasn't stood in front of me as I would have poked him with a stick to make sure he was awake."*

**Ollie, unimpressed by a linesman's performance at Bristol City**

# Ollie'
## isms

## -25-

*"I call us the Orange club – because our future's bright!"*

**Ollie's view on the upwardly mobile QPR**

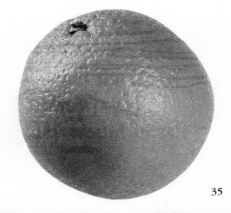

# -26-

"He's been out for a year and
Richard Langley is still six months
away from being Richard Langley,
and I could do with a fully fit
Richard Langley."

**Quiz: Which player is Ollie talking about?**

# Ollie'isms

## -27-

*"It's all very well having a great pianist playing but it's no good if you haven't got anyone to get the piano on the stage in the first place, otherwise the pianist would be standing there with no bloody piano to play."*

Ollie, in tune with the limitations of his Leicester City squad

# -28-

"*I am a football manager. I can't see into the future. Last year I thought I was going to Cornwall on my holidays but I ended up going to Lyme Regis.*"

**Ollie, in need of a SatNav and crystal ball**

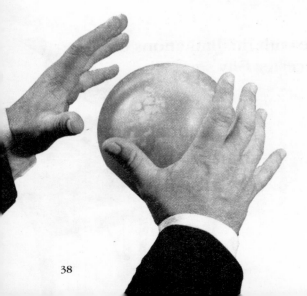

# Ollie'
## isms

# -29-

---

*"I always say that scoring goals is like driving a car. When the striker is going for goal, he's pushing down that accelerator, so the rest of the team has to come down off that clutch. If the clutch and the accelerator are down at the same time, then you are going to have an accident."*

**Ollie's steady road to success**

# -30-

*"I've got to knock that horrible smell out of my boys, because they smell of complacency."*

**Ollie suspects something fishy is going on within his Plymouth squad**

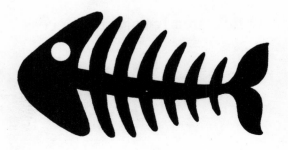

# Ollie'isms

## -31-

*"When my wife first saw Marc for the first time, she said he was a fine specimen of a man. She says I have nothing to worry about, but I think she wants me to buy her a QPR shirt with his name on the back for Christmas."*

**Danish striker Marc Nygaard attracting the wrong type of attention**

# -32-

---

*"Paul Furlong is my vintage Rolls Royce and he cost me nothing. We polish him, look after him, and I have him fine tuned by my mechanics. We take good care of him because we have to drive him every day, not just save him for weddings."*

**Veteran QPR striker Paul Furlong – blessed with a fine engine**

**Ollie explains:**
"Paul Furlong was getting older and older and I had to be really careful with him. I tried to use the analogy of a wedding car, meaning that if you drove it every day, it might not work as efficiently.

# Ollie'isms

I had masseurs, icepacks and physios working on him through the week just to keep him ticking along because I needed him on Saturdays and throughout the week. It's just about age and looking after yourself, really."

# -33-

*"Sometimes when you aim for the stars, you hit the moon."*

**Ollie could have been speaking about his mis-firing Leicester strikers' accuracy – but wasn't...**

# Ollie'isms

## -34-

*"I believe in what I am doing totally and once people speak to me they do too – I could sell snow to the Eskimos."*

**Ollie, focused and ice-cool**

# -35-

*"We've got a good squad and we're going to cut our cloth accordingly, but I think the cloth that we've got could make some good soup, if that makes any sense".*

Despite urban myths, Ollie was in fact misquoted as saying "soup" – he actually said "suit", though soup is more of an Ollie'ism…

# -36-

"*I want to try and spread the support with my Bristol connection. Rovers are in the bottom division so why can't I try and convert some of them into Argyle fans? We're in the West Country so it's not that far away. Only two and a half hours away in a slow car, an hour and a half in a fast one – or 10 minutes in a rocket! As long as you aimed it right, you'd be down here really quickly. Don't land it on the pitch, though, because you'd ruin it!*"

**Ollie's unsuccessful bid to fill Home Park with fellow Gasheads**

## -37-

*"It was a bit cheeky wasn't it? But I don't think it was that bad. It would have been worse if he'd turned round and dropped the front of his shorts instead. I don't think there's anything wrong with a couple of butt cheeks personally. If anybody's offended by seeing a backside, get real. Maybe they're just jealous that he's got a real nice tight one, with no cellulite or anything."*

Reaction to Manchester City midfielder Joey Barton 'mooning' incident at Goodison Park

# Ollie'isms

**Ollie explains:**

"I didn't agree with the stick Joey Barton got after he dropped his shorts for a split second. The kid was having enough problems, anyway, and I watched it and he was getting some abuse from the Everton fans when all he'd done was go over to give a disabled kid his shirt. All he did was show his arse to those who were giving him stick and I don't think anybody should really be offended by something like that. For the FA to try and then charge him with some kind of offence was ridiculous – I thought that at the time and I still think the same way now – so much so, that when I was at Plymouth, we cut out the ass of two pairs of shorts and stuck a plastic comedy ass out of each pair – one black, one white. Whichever player was voted the worst player of the week, they had to then wear the shorts with the ass cut out during training. Some clubs wear a yellow jersey, but each Friday, one of our lads would have to wear 'the Joey Barton shorts' as we called them!"

# -38-

*"Hasney's bust his hooter. He can smell round corners now."*

**Central defender Hasney Aljofree's nasal injury receives little sympathy…**

## -39-

*"Sir David Beckham? You're having a laugh. He's just a good footballer with a famous bird. Can you imagine if Posh was called Lady Beckham? We'd never hear the end of it!"*

**Rumours about a possible knighthood for David Beckham are met with short shrift**

## -40-

*"Have you ever seen The Incredibles? They have a kid and he's just so quick, like 'WHOOSH' and he's gone, and they call him 'Dash'.*

**Thoughts on the animated Scott Sinclair, then on loan at Plymouth from Chelsea**

# Ollie'isms

## -41-

*"And I think Mr. Incredible looks like Iain Dowie."*

**Ollie gives Iain Dowie his nicest-ever lookalike**

# -42-

*"If I was in there I wouldn't try to be everybody's friend. I'd have to say 'Excuse me, hang on a minute, I think you're wrong there. Don't raise your voice at her like that, don't get like that. It's just an Oxo cube, we got it wrong and we're all in this together'. It's like the Witches of Eastwick. They need Jack Nicholson to come in and sort them right out."*

Shilpa Shetty receives Ollie's backing after being bullied on Celebrity Big Brother 2007

# -43-

*"I've ridden a horse but I'm rubbish at it. I look like a crab sat on a horse with my hunched back. I've got rounded shoulders so I'm in all sorts of trouble and the bloody horse seems to know it as well! Many a time my wife's seen me in excruciating agony when I've gone down instead of going up – let's just say those bloody saddles are rather hard."*

**Equine trouble for Ollie? Neigh chance…**

## -44-

"*There was a woman in it who was quite well-endowed and two boys who used to get drunk and have a fight – it had everything for me.*"

**Ollie's thoughts on Dukes Of Hazzard – not an Oasis concert**

# Ollie'isms

## -45-

*"He is the oldest swinger in town but at this level he will add a touch of class."*

**Millwall-bound veteran midfielder Teddy Sheringham, whose false teeth glow in ultra-violet light, apparently**

# -46-

*"Did the dog know anything about this? And when they said 'I do', did she bark it out or what? I can't get over it – he should be locked up. And there's me thinking I'd seen it all on Jerry Springer when a bloke walked on and married this little horse. But this takes the biscuit – after stoning two poor dogs, he's allowed to marry another one. Very strange."*

**Ollie's answer to the oft-asked 'should humans be allowed to marry dogs' question**

**Ollie explains:** "I was fed a question for my BBC

website column and that was my reaction to it. I was horrified – did the dog know it was married and did it willingly say 'I do'? The only dog word I've ever heard is 'sausages'! Unbelieveable."

# -47-

*"I think us human beings will end up with thumbs like giant crabs pretty soon because of all the texting that goes on and the playing of these stupid computer games, and we'll have lost the art of talking. It really does worry me."*

Ollie – try calling him first…

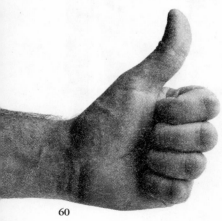

# -48-

*"If you go to the ballet you have about eight intervals – it's different class. In fact you could almost have your 10 pints during the breaks and by the end of it you're loving it. I strongly recommend it."*

**Ollie's puts a different slant on Swan Lake**

# -49-

*"Grease… What a great movie. When Olivia Neutron Bomb comes on in that tight gear at the end it's scary isn't it? When she changes from nice little Sandy into a hellcat on legs... whoah! Unbelievable."*

**Ollie, shaping up for Olivia**

# Ollie'
### isms

## -50-

*"Favourite Bond villain? I like Oddjob, remember him? He was the sidekick of somebody. I like the way he threw that hat and knocked the thing off."*

**Ollie, who admits to having one or two odd jobs himself over the years**

# -51-

*"I would like nothing more than to be like the rest of my family and chill out over Christmas, have a nice little snooze in the afternoon, eat a little bit too much, drink the odd thing that is a bit "ooh wait a minute", then on Boxing Day watch a lovely film on the telly – Chitty Chitty Bang Bang or something – and have a game of charades."*

**An unimpressed Ollie, prior to Plymouth's 2006 festive programme**

**Ollie explains:** "I tried to paint the archetypical

family Christmas, not including the bit where you have a row with the missus about getting her the wrong present and the kids screaming and fighting about who plays with what. I tried to make it a nice family scenario because us football people don't actually know what it's like to have a family Christmas because we're off training or driving miles to a hotel to stay overnight somewhere. It was all about what I'd like to do at Christmas as opposed to what I actually had to do, which was go in at 8.30am and organise training or whatever. When I was at QPR as a player, I had to leave my home in Bristol at 6am, drive the four hours it took to get to London and back – so most of my day was spent doing an impression of Chris Rea – driving home for Christmas!"

# -52-

*'I think it's a pile of donkey dung. FIFA should scrap the Bosman ruling and get back to the way it was where anybody who is out of contract should be owned by the club and he should be able to command a fee for them.'*

**Ollie offers a restrained opinion on FIFA's transfer policies**

**Ollie explains:**
"The Bosman Ruling is the worst law in the world. A player who is over 24 walks away for nothing with no benefit to the club whatsoever. If people want freedom of movement, if they're good enough, they'll move on anyway. They'll either be out of contract or a price will be paid for their

services – if a player breaks his leg and they've run out of contract with the intention of signing for someone else, they could become unemployable because of the Bosman Ruling. I think it's a big pile of steaming you-know-what."

# -53-

*"I've been polishing that car since I've been here. Unfortunately, I didn't buy it off the forecourt straight away… I'm not going to spend all this time polishing that car and then let somebody rip it away from me off my drive in the summer for absolutely nothing. That's bad business. Somebody is going to have to buy it off me, and I might have to push it off my drive if it doesn't want to go."*

**The car in question – Tony Capaldi – was later towed to Cardiff City**

# -54-

"As a player Roy Keane was awesome – and hard as nails. You wouldn't mess with him. A running machine, a tackling machine – a winning machine. He was like a shark in the middle of the pitch. There was nothing of him but if you clattered into him it was like hitting the side of a train. I just couldn't live with him.'

**Ollie on the Jaws-dropping talent of Keano**

# -55-

*"Ha ha! Well that's very flattering but I think they'll have to go and swivel on that idea!"*

**Ollie's reaction to the possibility of being offered the England job**

*Ollie'isms*

## -56-

"*If that's a penalty, then I may as well say I'm Alec McJockstrap and wear a kilt.*"

Ollie scotches a referee's decision against Southampton, 2007

71

## -57-

---

*"I rung Kenny Jackett straight away to congratulate him on getting Swansea promoted and he said, 'I'm waiting to get my goalie out of jail'. You can't even celebrate these days, can you?"*

**Ollie and a straight Jackett?**

# -58-

*"Leicester City is a marvellous club and I am as devastated as anybody that this great club suffered relegation. I gave 100 per cent to the cause but unfortunately we ran out of time."*

**Ollie's forlorn race against the clock at The Walkers Stadium**

# -59-

---

*"If I hadn't done that programme, I wouldn't be sitting here now. Before I did it, I believed that I was a person who was kind, considerate, and believed in free speech. The anger management expert showed me I was a jumped-up, obnoxious little git who wouldn't listen at home because of what happened at work. If I'd carried on the way I was, I would have destructed everything I had."*

Ollie, post 'Stress Test'

# -60-

*"My arms withered and my body was covered with puss-like sores, but no matter how bad it got I consoled myself by remembering that I wasn't a Chelsea fan."*

**Ollie rules himself out of any future Stamford Bridge vacancies**

**Ollie explains:**
"I said that after we'd lost the play-off final with QPR. I nicked that one off Marc Bircham, in all honesty, because he's a fanatical QPR fan and he said that on the coach home after the play-off defeat."

# -61-

"*When I was at Bristol Rovers,*" *he says,* "*there was a journalist who wrote a match report where he said that if Bristol City had my two strikers – who, in that game, were rubbish – then City would be a team Bristol could be proud of. Oooof! I got him to the training ground.*

*He didn't know why. I said: 'You are going to apologise to my team, you bastard.' I sat all my players down. I had the two centre halves stand up. I said: 'Right, now tell these two – who you only gave five out of 10 each – just how well you think they played, you asshole.'"*

**Note to journos: lowest mark must be six…**

# -62-

*"We are an offshoot of apes –
allegedly – but who knows? We
don't really, do we? How long have
we been on this planet? How long
are we going to be here? What is it
all about? We reproduce.
Our offspring carry on. But that
will only happen for a limited time.
Before the whole thing blows up
and we are sucked into a black
hole. You know what I mean?"*

**Ollie, apparently not in one of his
chirpier moments**

# -63-

"*We've got to go there and tweak the nose of fear and stick an ice cube down the vest of terror. That's not an Ian Holloway quote, by the way. It's Blackadder.*"

**Ollie tries to smile prior to Leicester's do-or-die visit to Stoke, May 2008**

# -64-

*"If Sven-Goran Eriksson can get the sack after the results he has had, then who am I? If Jose Mourinho can be sacked and Avram Grant is in a European Cup final and might be sacked, then who am I?"*

**Ollie on the crazy world of football management**

**Ollie explains:**
"That was about the general madness in football. People were talking to me about Leicester and how I felt about just arriving in the job. I said, 'What does that matter?', meaning that it doesn't matter how long you've been in a job, with the way things are going, what chance do you really get anyway?"

# -65-

"*Statistically, I'm currently the worst Leicester City manager in history and that doesn't sit well with me. On my gravestone it will say, 'Here lies Ollie – he tried.' I will never give up*"

And he never will....

# -66-

*"We've got Leicester on Saturday and they've sacked Martin Allen, their manager, which was a bit of a strange state of affairs – especially after they'd just beaten Watford 4-1. That'll teach him!"*

Ollie preps his Plymouth side prior to a visit to the East Midlands

# -67-

"He signed while I was still manager at QPR. He was a wonderful kid, irrespective of what he could do on a football pitch. He was someone I would have been proud to call my son. He was respectful, a wonderful lad with a brilliant smile. The room lit up when he came into it. He was one of those people. My heart bleeds for his parents. He's going to be sorely missed to the world, not just his mum and dad. The world was a better place with him in it."

**Ollie, on the tragic death of young QPR star Ray Jones**

# -68-

*"If my aunty had balls, she'd be my uncle!"*

## A simple, but poignant observation by a philosophical Ollie

**Ollie explains:** "This was one of my dad's favourite sayings and it basically means, 'don't make excuses, son!' I once said, 'yeah, but if I had long hair, I'd be a rock star.' It's a response to any ifs, buts or maybe-type remarks that are thrown my way and I think it does the job."

# *Ollie'*
## *isms*

# -69-

---

*"Do you believe everything you read in The Sun? They've got some nice tits in that paper."*

**Ollie suggests being linked with the Millwall job might not be true**

# -70-

*"Most of our fans get behind us and are fantastic but those who don't should shut the hell up or they can come round to my house and I will fight them."*

**Ollie on Loftus Road's more negative fans**

# -71-

*"Everyone calls him a gypsy but
I can assure you he doesn't live
in a caravan. He has a house
with foundations."*

**Ollie comments on the abuse Gino Padula
was receiving from away fans**

# -72-

---

*"When you play with wingers you look a bit like a taxi with both doors open, anyone can get in or out. "*

**Ollie hails a fare poor performance during a pre-season friendly**

# Ollie'isms

## -73-

*"In football, there is no definite lifespan or time span for a manager. After a while you start smelling of fish. The other week it looked like I was stinking of Halibut!"*

**Ollie trawls for reasoning behind QPR's bad start to the season**

# -74-

*"I'm fed up with my career going backwards because my team has been sold from underneath my nose. Before I die I wanted to have the chance to spend some money. There was a bomb ticking and if it had gone off and somebody else had got the job I would always have felt the bridesmaid. The game, the business, stinks sometimes but I don't. I would have been a liar if I had stayed at Plymouth."*

Ollie's honest response to why he quit
Home Park for Leicester

# Ollie'
## isms

## -75-

*"I feel like I have been acting in Coronation Street all my life and now I am King Lear. I just felt I couldn't turn this down. I can't wait to get started. This is a whole new challenge which throws me into a whole new ball park."*

**Ollie on accepting Milan Mandaric's offer to manage the Foxes**

# -76-

*"I'm all geared up for the Derby game. I'm looking forward to it although it's raining heavily down here at the moment. I haven't quite finished my ark yet, so it's a bit worrying. But we've got our water wings and a rubber ring ready and Derby don't know about that so we've got one up on them already."*

**Ollie gives his quotes two-by-two**

**Ollie explains:**
"That came from the fact that it had rained so much in the days leading up to our cup-tie with Derby County, we were half expecting to see Noah roll up in Plymouth town centre. The pitch at

# Ollie'isms

Home Park was so sodden and boggy, we almost needed a boat to go and play. As it was, we won the game and moved into the FA Cup quarter-final."

# -77-

*"I went out for a meal with my good lady to a wonderful Indian restaurant down here and we had a bottle of champagne. I didn't buy her any flowers because she didn't want any. She was lucky to get the meal, but I suppose I was lucky she didn't go to the opticians so she can see what I really look like! I always keep her away from there. Every time she wants to go the opticians I say "no, you don't need to go in there, love!" and turn and walk the other way."*

**Mrs Holloway nee Magoo, according to her husband**

# -78-

"I've broken them all already! I wasn't gonna swear this year and I ruined that on New Year's Day by swearing at the fourth official. I was devastated at the end – not because we didn't win the game or that the ref cancelled out our goal, or that he should have cancelled their goal, or that he sent my centre forward off for deliberate handball which wasn't deliberate at all. Nothing to do with any of that – it was the fact that I swore at the fourth official about the linesman on the other side. So that's one New

*Year's resolution gone and the second one went that night when I was a bit down and had one glass of wine too many. So what a terrible New Year I'm having! I wasn't going to drink for at least a month and I was going to get fit and all that and I've blown it."*

**Vive la resolution! New Year 2007**

# -79-

*"The result is sometimes in the lap of the Gods. But I will prepare to try and win the game. My record over the years has been shocking. I'm like a cheap tea bag – I don't stay long in the Cup!"*

**Something brewing when Ollie's in the FA Cup…**

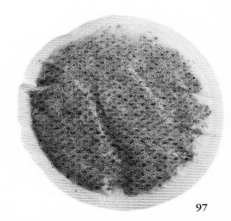

# -80-

*"I'm not tempted to put the boots on again, ever. But then Hessie's a lot fitter than I am. He never used to be but he is now. We should check him to make sure he's not an alien because that bloke's just superhuman. I reckon if you cut him up the middle there's going to be a little alien holding up a stick like on Men in Black! Steward's inquiry on Andy Hessenthaler – is he human?"*

**Ollie on Andy Hessenthaler,
still playing at 42**

# -81-

"I lost to Vauxhall Motors in the
Cup on penalties – now you don't
get much more embarrassing than
that because their name is
atrocious isn't it? It sounded like
we were beaten by a car. We didn't
get into first gear and were
automatically knocked out of the
Cup. It meant that much that a taxi
driver who is now a good friend of
mine came in and spoke to me for
two hours about what I should
have done. But then I looked at the
team he would have picked and I
said, 'They're all bloody injured,

*you complete pillock' He didn't realise how hard it was being a football manager."*

Ollie leaves tips of a different kind...

# -82-

*"It's still in my body and I'll have to pass it at sometime but my passing's absolutely diabolical. That's what I told the doctor: 'What chance have I got of passing anything – did you see me play?!' When it happened I was lying on the floor of my office in pain thinking this place isn't very clean – the carpet needs changing, the walls need painting... and when I got up I was covered in rubbish. If I want to be in the Premier League one day, I should be able to roll around in agony on my floor*

*without getting dirty. So I'm going to order a new carpet and some paint for my office. There's always something good that comes out of something bad."*

**Ollie explains problems at the back**

# Ollie'isms

## -83-

*"Why would I sell him and why would he want to go to a club like that? They strut around as if they are a big club, but they ain't. Southampton have come in twice now and I've told them to piss off both times. They won't be coming back, I can promise you."*

**Ollie strengthens the south-coast relationship between Plymouth and Southampton, 2006**

**Ollie explains:**
"That was because Southampton were doing things and saying things in the press about David Norris, trying to unsettle him. I didn't like it at all

so I let them know about it – clubs like that think they can do things like that – I wanted to let them know I wasn't going to take it."

# Ollie'isms

## -84-

*"I'm sick and tired of every Tom, Dick and Harry getting linked with my job every day. Well ding, dang, doo. It's my job, I own it and it's up to anyone else to take it off me."*

**Ollie fends off would-be suitors for his job at Loftus Road, Dec 2005**

### Ollie explains:

"I wanted to actually swap 'ding dang doo' for f**k the lot of you! Of course, I couldn't, so made do with that instead. Martin Jol must have got sick of the same situation when he was Spurs manager where every single day somebody was being linked with his job. At QPR, there was constant speculation about John Gregory and Jim Smith and god-knows-who else and there is hardly ever smoke without fire. It was my way of saying that it was my job and it was up to somebody to tell me otherwise."

# Ollie'isms

## -85-

*"I couldn't be more chuffed if I were a badger at the start of the mating season."*

Ollie, good for a quote, when badgered

# -86-

*"I needed a bigger garden. I only had a little one. I told my wife after a week I was knackered. I tried to help by pulling out weeds, and it turned out they were her plants! She wasn't very happy!"*

**On gardening leave at QPR**

# -87-

*"We looked more like Queens Park
Strangers out there."*

**Commenting on the five debutants Ollie had
starting at Leeds**

# -88-

*"I watched Arsenal in the Champions League the other week playing some of the best football I've ever seen and yet they couldn't have scored in a brothel with two grand in their pockets!"*

**On Arsenal failing to take their chances – on the pitch**

# Ollie'isms

## -89-

*"I was never tempted to become a punk. I was Sidney Serious, I was into George Benson. I was smooth. Smooth as a cashmere codpiece."*

**Ollie, The Codfather of sole.**

# -90-

"*I've never had a bet myself; I wouldn't know how to put one on. I've never seen a rich gambler and I've never seen a broke bookie either. I want to become addicted to a lot of things, but not gambling. I'm addicted to my wife, though – I can't leave her alone!*"

**Ollie, at odds with gambling**

# Ollie'isms

## -91-

*"If I'd have been one of their fans I'd have hit him with a bottle myself."*

**Ollie reacts to an over-the-top goal celebration by his own player**

# -92-

*"I love the big man, absolutely brilliant. Some of the films were a bit dodgy. That one where he was diving off a cliff, he climbed back up to the top, his hair was immaculate and he wasn't even wet... and for me that's why he's the King."*

**Ollie on Elvis, not Barry Hayles**

**Ollie explains:**
"Yeah, this was about 'Elv the Pelv'. There was one film where he was doing cliff-diving and he climbed out of the water and was bone dry with perfect hair – was that a plastic hat he used to wear or was it real? Maybe he had the original

version you can buy in joke shops with the
sideburns and the quiff!"

# -93-

*"We are all going to walk across a pit of coals and someone will teach us how to do it. I hope they will because I can't even walk on hot sand. It's all about training you to be a better person. Mastering your mind and focusing on the right things are important skills to have. There are millions of people who can kick a ball around but only a few can do it under pressure. You have to block out everything and focus on the game."*

The philosopher speaks…

*Ollie'*
*isms*

# -94-

*"When their man was sent off, it seemed to wake up the crowd and give them someone to get their teeth into and fortunately for us that was the referee."*

**Official response works in Ollie's favour...**

## -95-

*"He's six-foot something, fit as a flea, good-looking – he's got to have something wrong with him."*

**Ollie, when asked his opinion on Cristiano Ronaldo, prior to the Champions League Final 2008**

# -96-

*"My day didn't start very well.... the Holloway household had to have our dog put down unfortunately, but that's life. I've just said to the lads: 'You're born and you die on a date. You've got to work on the dash in the middle'....."*

**Ollie on a Dog Day Afternoon**

# -97-

---

*"If you can keep your noses in front at the end, that's what counts. It's been said that I have a bit of a Roman nose and I am keeping it ahead at the moment. Hopefully it's all about the length of your hooter because I might be in front at the end of the season as well!"*

**He nose his stuff you know…**

# -98-

*"I've had a week from hell, I'm trying to learn how to relax. I'm now going to enjoy this, take my brain out and stick it in an ice bucket."*

## QPR's 4-1 at Hartlepool gets an icy response

**Ollie explains:**
"Doing the job I was doing at QPR. I hardly ever had free thoughts. I'd be sat down eating my tea and my kids or my wife would be talking to me and I'd be mentally elsewhere, thinking about my job. It invaded every waking moment and I was just trying to say that it would be nice to shut down the computer, stick my brain in an ice bucket so it'd come out nice and cool instead of feeling red hot all the time. I think that's an analogy we can all relate to sometimes, not just football managers."

# -99-

*"Look at the prickly little fella down the road at Chelsea. He wants to win everything and we can learn from that. If there were two flies crawling up the wall he'd be desperate to back the winner."*

**Ollie on The Special One's competitive nature**

**Ollie explains:**
"This quote is about winning. When I first arrived at QPR as a player and then as a manager, there was an attitude of 'oh well, we can win next week'. I was trying to focus on the bloke down the road at Stamford Bridge who was a winner and wanted to win every game he was involved with and that's what life is all about, really. You have to have that mentality because although you can't always win

# Ollie'isms

every time, you have to want to because I think wanting to makes all the difference."

# -100-

## Ollie's Favourite Quote

*"To put it in gentleman's terms, if you've been out for a night and you're looking for a young lady and you pull one, you've done what you set out to do. We didn't look our best today but we've pulled. Some weeks the lady is good looking and some weeks they're not. Our performance today would have been not the best looking bird but at least we got her in the taxi. She may not have been the best looking lady we ended up*

# Ollie'isms

*taking home but it was still very pleasant and very nice, so thanks very much and let's have coffee. "*

**Ollie explains:**

"You'd maybe guess this was my favourite! I think this will be forever associated with my outlook on football and life and how the two have many situations that cross over and can be compared. I used to say the same thing to players and they used to love it. One day I was waffling on in a press conference and it just sort of came out. I think the journalists wondered – 'did he really just say that?' and they asked me to elaborate on it. By the time I'd explained what I meant, I was thinking 'God, I'm going to be in trouble with my wife, here,' – and I was! She wasn't very happy when she read it and said 'You didn't pull me like that.' I think everyone plays those games, though – women and men – where they might end up with an ugly one in the taxi but they still have a coffee with them and away they go!"

# Also available:

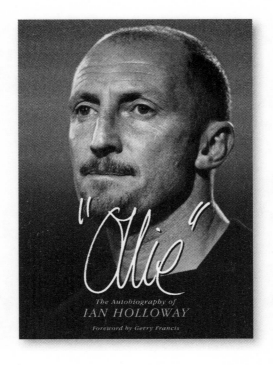

*From all good stockists*